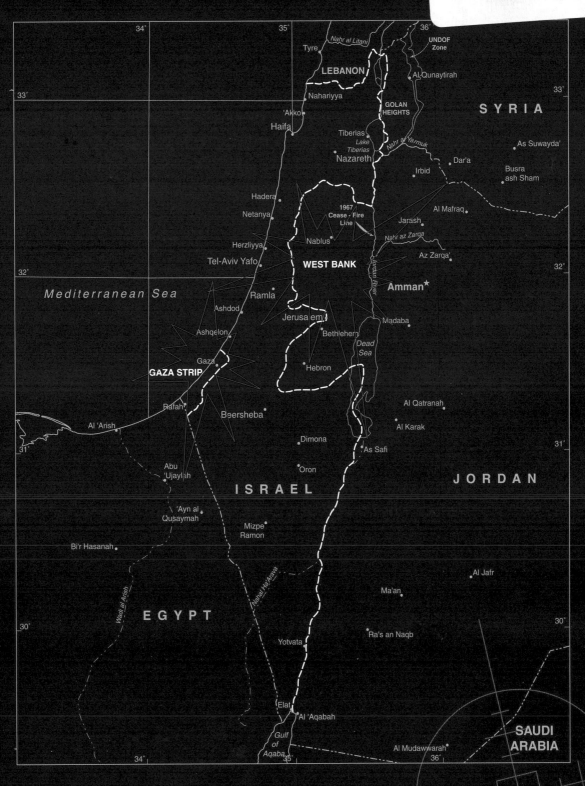

DAYS OF CHANGE

Creative Education

BY RACHAEL HANEL

Published by Creative Education
P.O. Box 227, Mankato, Minnesota 56002
Creative Education is an imprint of The Creative Company.

Cover design and art direction by Rita Marshall
Interior design and book production by The Design Lab
Printed in the United States of America

Photographs by Alamy (Mary Evans Picture Library, POP-
PERFOTO, Trip, Visual Arts Library), Corbis (Shawn Baldwin,
Bettmann, John Garett), Getty Images (AFP, Aurora, Hulton
Archive, Imagno, David Silverman, Time Life Pictures)

Library of Congress Cataloging-in-Publication Data
Hanel, Rachael.
The Israeli-Palestinian conflict / by Rachael Hanel.
p. cm. – (Days of change)
Includes bibliographical references and index.
ISBN-13: 978-1-58341-548-1
1. Arab-Israeli conflict–1993–Peace–Juvenile literature. I. Title.
DS119.76.H35675 2007
956.9405'4–dc22   2006020148

First edition
9 8 7 6 5 4 3 2 1

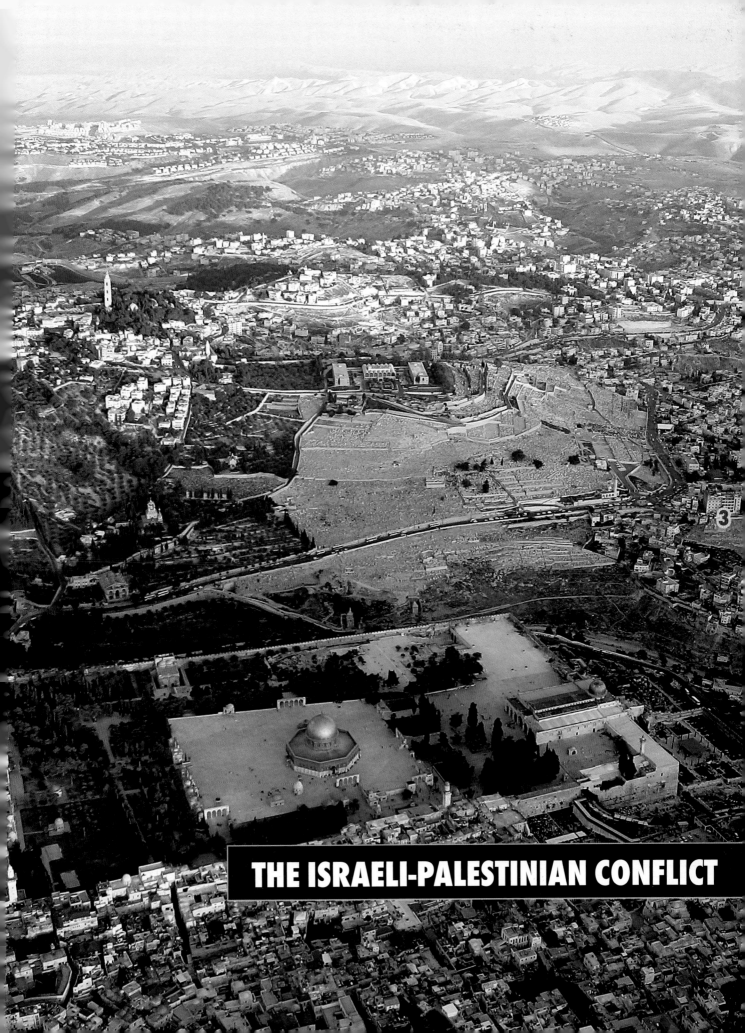

THE ISRAELI-PALESTINIAN CONFLICT

In 1993, Bill Clinton (center) stood by as Yitzhak Rabin (left) of Israel and Yasser Arafat of Palestine shook hands, vowing to work toward a peace that has not yet been reached.

On September 13, 1993, the world witnessed a moment that many people had thought impossible. At the White House, with

United States President Bill Clinton looking on, representatives of two sworn and bitter enemies—Israel and Palestine—shook hands. The government of Israel, led by Yitzhak Rabin, and the Palestinian Liberation Organization, headed by Yasser Arafat, had reached a peace accord after decades of war. At the signing ceremony, Arafat was the first to extend his hand. Rabin hesitated, at first unwilling to return the gesture, but soon reached for Arafat's hand and even formed a slight smile.

Unfortunately, the hopeful moment was fleeting, as the agreement did not solve the intense problems between Jews and Arabs. Further peace talks were attempted but fell through. In 2000, Israeli Prime Minister-elect Ariel Sharon, whom many Palestinians viewed as having played an integral role in previous violence, visited a holy site in East Jerusalem revered by both Muslims and Jews, an action that helped to set off a new wave of Palestinian *intifada*, or violent uprising. Today, the world continues to seek an answer to this tightly concentrated conflict of religion, nationality, ethnicity, and culture—a conflict in which both sides fight over territory and security, each claiming the role of victim and seeking land as its reward.

The Israeli-Palestinian conflict pits Jews against Arabs. Both Israel and Palestine are ancient, neighboring territories of the Middle East. The Bible refers to Israel many times as "The Promised Land," a region God pledged to the Jews. Both Arabs and Jews trace their lineage back to Abraham, a prophet of the Bible's Old Testament, who lived in ancient Israel. For this reason, both sides claim this small area of land as their own.

Jews lived in the area now known as Israel in large numbers until A.D. 70, when Roman conquerors destroyed the Jewish temple in Jerusalem and drove out the Jews, resulting in a massive exodus known as the *Diaspora*. From there, Jews emigrated to different parts of the world. However, some Jews remained, at times resisting both Muslim and Christian conquerors. Arabs, too, spread outward from the Middle East after the Islamic religion was founded in A.D. 622. Arabs live all over the world but are concentrated in Middle Eastern and north African countries. They are an ethnic group, and not all ethnic Arabs are Muslim—some are Christians, and a tiny minority are even Jews.

AN OPPRESSED HISTORY

For centuries, Jews and Arabs—specifically Palestinians—have been the victims of oppression. In the Middle Ages, Europeans viewed Jews as an inferior people and often pushed them into separate living areas called ghettos. This treatment continued for centuries and escalated dramatically in the 20th century during World War II. After most Jews left the Middle East during the Diaspora, Palestine—the land

Jerusalem is sacred to both Jews and Muslims. The second king of ancient Israel, David, made the city the capital of his kingdom around 900 B.C. For Muslims, Jerusalem was where the prophet Muhammad took a mystical night journey to the Temple Mount, where he ascended to heaven to gain a vision of Allah. Jerusalem is home to the Western Wall, a remnant of the most holy Jewish temple in that city, as well as Al-Aqsa mosque and Dome of the Rock, revered by Arabs. Although the partition of 1947 called for Jerusalem to be an international city, peace talks have often broken down over which side will control these holy sites.

Like Muslims and Jews, Christians consider Jerusalem sacred; in 1099, Christian crusaders took over the city, slaughtering many of its Muslim inhabitants.

the Jews called home in ancient times—was comprised of a largely Arabic population. These Arabs lived under various rulers during times when vast empires spanned the Eastern Hemisphere. From 1516 to 1918, the Ottoman Empire—centered in present-day Turkey—occupied Palestine and ruled its people. Shortly before World War I began in 1914, a wave of nationalism spread among Palestinians, who began to clamor for an independent state.

Around the same time, a movement called Zionism, led by an Austrian Jew named Theodor Herzl, gathered momentum in Europe. At the beginning of the 20th century, Jews still faced persecution from the Christian majority, and many desired their own nation, a place where their population would be in the majority. Jews soon looked to Palestine as this land. Although the realization of this dream was still nearly 50 years away, they decided they would call it Israel, a place that would allow the rebirth of a Jewish culture.

An initial wave of *aliyah* (the Hebrew word for "going up"), or Jewish immigration to Palestine, had already occurred in 1881. And just prior to World War I, the separate visions of Jews and Arabs living in Palestine began to collide, as each group dreamed of creating its own state on

"We have been granted the great privilege of witnessing this victory for peace. Just as the Jewish people this week celebrate the dawn of a new year, let us all go from this place to celebrate the dawn of a new era—not only for the Middle East, but for the entire world."

PRESIDENT BILL CLINTON, at the signing of the Israel-PLO peace accord, September 13, 1993

Theodor Herzl is considered the father of modern Zionism. Herzl, a Jewish Austrian journalist, famously put his ideas forth in his 1896 book *Der Judenstaat* ("The Jewish State"). In it, he urged Jews to act as one people who deserved their own country, stating that they could gain acceptance and strength if they drew together as one rather than living as minorities in separate countries. Herzl championed Zionism throughout the world, and his followers held international meetings and raised money to further their cause. Herzliya, a town just north of Tel Aviv in Israel, was named after Herzl.

Theodor Herzl believed that a homeland was critical to Jews' welfare, once writing, "Above all, I recognized the emptiness and futility of trying to 'combat' anti-Semitism."

In Europe, Jews witnessed many acts of anti-Semitism over the course of centuries. One infamous incident was the Dreyfus Affair in France in 1894. A Jewish officer in the French military, Alfred Dreyfus, was charged with distributing military secrets and convicted of treason. Mass rallies against Dreyfus were held in the streets of Paris, where people chanted "Death to the Jews!" Dreyfus was sentenced to life in a penal colony and served five years before his conviction was overturned. For many Jews, this incident was the last straw. Weary of anti-Semitism, many turned their thoughts to Zionism and the idea of having their own country, Israel.

Chaim Weizmann (third from left), who would become Israel's first president, was one of the leaders of the Zionist movement and worked with Britain on the Balfour Declaration.

the same land—an area roughly the size of Massachusetts. Britain soon stepped in to help mediate the conflict. During World War I, Britain was a powerful country that had taken a special interest in Palestine. The Middle East contained rich oil reserves, and Palestine was a vital link in trade routes between Europe and Asia.

The British saw the creation of a national state for Jews—many of whom had close ties to Europe—in Palestine as a means of increasing Britain's influence in the strategically important region. To further this effort as peaceably as possible, British governmental officials proposed ideas about how Palestine should be divided, making pledges and agreements—some public, others secret—to both Jews and Arabs. The last of these World War I-era agreements was the 1917 Balfour

Although a second trial in 1899 again found Alfred Dreyfus guilty, the verdict was overturned 10 days later, freeing Dreyfus; later that year, the true spy confessed.

Declaration, which stated, "His Majesty's Government views with favour the establishment in Palestine of a national home for Jewish people . . . it being clearly understood that nothing shall be done which may prejudice the civil and religious rights of existing non-Jewish communities in Palestine. . . ."

After World War I ended in 1918 with the defeat of Germany, Austria-Hungary, and the Ottomans, the victorious nations of Britain and France split land in the Middle East into mandates. Palestine became a British mandate, meaning that Britain would control the region until Palestinians could become organized enough to rule it themselves. The Balfour Declaration went into effect, and Jews already living in Palestine quickly created their own educational and health care systems.

After the Balfour Declaration, Palestine witnessed spurts of violence in the form of anti-Jewish riots and occasional attacks upon Jewish settlements, as Palestinians viewed with resentment these new settlers who were so quick to establish their own customs and religion. In 1936, an Arab rebellion escalated tensions dramatically. For three years, Arabs protested the notion of a Jewish state and expressed their opposition to the British policy that allowed Jews into the country by refusing to pay taxes

"We will need more courage and determination to continue the course of building coexistence and peace between us. This is possible and it will happen with mutual determination and with the effort that will be made with all parties on all the tracks to establish the foundations of a just and comprehensive peace."

PLO CHAIRMAN YASSER ARAFAT, at the signing of the Israel-PLO peace accord, September 13, 1993

12

In 1925, a large crowd gathered at a new Jewish university in Palestine to welcome British cabinet member Arthur Balfour, who had penned the Balfour Declaration.

"Oppression and
persecution cannot
exterminate us.
No nation on
earth has survived
such struggles and
sufferings as we have
gone through. . . .
No one can deny
the gravity of the
situation of the Jews.
Where they live in
perceptible numbers,
they are more or less
persecuted."

THEODOR HERZL,
leader of the Zionist
movement, 1896

Nazi dictator Adolf Hitler

or recognize British government offices. The rebellion hinted at the increased violence to come, as some Arabs began launching guerrilla attacks in efforts to kill British officials and Jews.

In 1939, British officials suggested the idea of partition as a way to curb the rising violence and find a solution that would appeal to both sides. With partition, Jews and Arabs would have separate states within Palestine. Britain issued a formal declaration, known as the 1939 White Paper, in which it tried to gain favor with Arabs by limiting further Jewish immigration and severely cutting back on land sales to Jews, actions that seemed to roll back the freedoms granted Jews in the 1917 Balfour Declaration. While the White Paper was widely seen as an olive branch to Palestine's Arabs, it left Jews dismayed.

The outbreak of World War II in 1939 put all deals on hold. The most horrifying event in Jewish history—the Holocaust—occurred during the war at the hands of the German Nazi party. Nazi dictator Adolf Hitler called for the extermination of the Jews, an order that stemmed from the age-old belief among some Europeans that Jews were inferior to the Caucasian race physically and mentally. Hitler saw Jews (along with other groups such as Gypsies and homosexuals) as pollutants to the human race and sought to eliminate them. From

15

During World War II, Jews were under constant threat from the Nazis, who forced them into ghettos and sent them to extermination camps, where many were gassed to death.

1933 to 1945, the Nazis systematically murdered six million Jews—one-third of the world's Jewish population—in concentration camps scattered throughout the German, Polish, and Austrian countrysides.

After World War II ended in 1945 with the downfall of Nazi Germany, surviving Jews poured into displaced persons camps throughout Europe. Most could not return to their previous lives, as their homes, schools, and synagogues had been destroyed. In the face of this need for homes and healing, the desire for a Jewish state grew among Holocaust survivors. Much of the world was left horrified by the Holocaust, and giving Jews their own state in a former Jewish land was seen by many as a way to help make up for the atrocities they had suffered.

The U.S., which emerged from World War II a global superpower, gave support to the idea of creating a Jewish state, partly as a means of building security in the Middle East, as America also recognized the political importance of Palestine and the surrounding region. However, Britain and the U.S. could not come up with a reasonable solution for splitting territory between Arabs and Jews, so in 1947, they turned the issue over to

"Let me say to you, the Palestinians, we are destined to live together on the same soil in the same land. We, the soldiers who have returned from battles stained with blood; we who have seen our relatives and friends killed before our eyes; we who have attended their funerals and cannot look into the eyes of their parents; we who have come from a land where parents bury their children; we who have fought against you, the Palestinians, we say to you today in a loud and a clear voice, enough of blood and tears. Enough!"

ISRAELI PRIME MINISTER YITZHAK RABIN, at the signing of the Israel-PLO peace accord, September 13, 1993

16

After World War II, Britain, still in control of Palestine, limited Jewish immigration to the area in an effort to appease Arabs, who protested the number of immigrant arrivals. Officials ordered all ships that reached Palestine carrying illegal immigrants to turn around. The first ship to test this rule was the *Exodus*. The *Exodus* left France in 1947 with more than 4,500 Jews, most lacking immigration certificates. British ships followed the defiant *Exodus* on its journey, and at the shores of Palestine ordered the people to return to France. Eventually, the passengers were forced to disembark in Germany, but many ended up later settling in Israel.

יציאת אירופה

After the Holocaust, many Jewish survivors—some still in their concentration camp uniforms—headed to Palestine hoping to find a new life and, ultimately, a new homeland.

a newly created world body, the United Nations (UN).

The first-ever session held by the UN in 1947 considered the issue of Palestine. After several debates, the UN approved a partition plan that created borders for Israel and designated areas for Palestinians. The western coast of Palestine and the Negev Desert region would become Israel, while Palestine would consist of Gaza and the West Bank of the Jordan River. Under the partition plan, Palestinians were allotted 4,500 square miles (11,665 sq km), while the new Jewish state occupied 5,500 square miles (14,245 sq km). On May 14, 1948, the state of Israel was declared.

When the state of Israel was created in 1948, millions of Palestinians were forced from their homes. They flooded into neighboring Arab countries, and the UN set up camps for these refugees. Today, approximately 4.3 million Palestinians—refugees and their descendents—are registered with the UN Relief and Works Agency for Palestine Refugees in the Near East (UNWRA), which is responsible for overseeing the refugee program. Jordan today hosts the most refugees—about 1.8 million. Israel maintains that allowing the refugees to return would upset the demographic balance of its state, while Palestinians argue they have the right to return to their ancestral homeland.

Despite the fact that the UN partition gave control of the West Bank to Palestine, the area is today occupied by Israel, although most of its settlers are Palestinians.

Israel's new statehood was greeted with violence from the Arab world, as the Israeli War of Independence broke out immediately after the nation of Israel was declared. Five Arab nations (Egypt, Transjordan, Syria, Lebanon, and Iraq) attacked Israel, which fought back using weapons obtained from Czechoslovakia and other countries. When the war ended a few months later after the deaths of 6,000 Israelis and as many as 15,000 Arabs, Palestinians had lost even more. Israel had claimed more territory, increasing its area by 20 percent over the UN partition, while Transjordan (later Jordan) annexed what had been Palestine's West Bank, and Egypt controlled Gaza—developments that forced thousands of Palestinians from their homes into refugee camps.

CONSTANT CONFLICT

Although Israel had gained territory, it felt unsafe, for Arab states bordered it on all sides. Arab leaders such as Gamal Abdul Nasser of Egypt opposed Israel's statehood and strongly believed in Arab nationalism. He and other leaders of the region envisioned a new coalition of Arab states that would drive Westerners—primarily Americans, Israelis, and the British—out of Arab lands.

Accordingly, in 1956, Nasser decided to take back the Suez Canal from the British, who had claimed the important waterway decades earlier. The canal served as a vital thoroughfare from the Mediterranean Sea to the Red Sea, making travel from Europe to Asia easy and affordable. Nasser's intentions caused great concern in Israel, as Israelis relied on use of

Jews faced threats and grief immediately in their new homeland; thousands of killed Israeli soldiers were buried in the first three months of Israel's existence in 1948.

the canal for commerce and trade. Suspecting that Egypt was preparing for an attack on their state, Israelis continued fortifying their defenses in the form of French fighter jets and other arms.

In October 1956, Israel launched a preemptive strike against Egypt with the support of the British and French. In what became known as the Suez War, Israel conquered Gaza and the entire Sinai Peninsula all the way to the canal (although it would bow to international pressure and return Sinai and Gaza a year later). After the week-long battle, the Arab world looked upon Britain and France with disdain for the stand they took with Israel. The U.S. stepped in, hoping to mediate the conflict, but many Arabs viewed America's efforts, too, as pro-Israeli. Although defeated, Nasser and his allies were praised as heroes in the Arab world

Throughout most of its history, Israel has relied on a citizen army for defense, both in times of relative calm and in times of war. The Israel Defense Force (IDF) consists of an army, navy, and air force. Most men and women enter the IDF at age 18. Women serve for two years, men for three (with men usually serving another couple of decades as reserve troops). The mandatory enrollment can be exempted for many reasons, including religious study, but is a necessary law to keep the small nation of seven million people strong militarily. Arab Israeli citizens are exempted from compulsory service but can volunteer.

Despite the Israeli invasion of their land in 1956, Arab fishermen on the Mediterranean coast in Gaza continued to focus on making a living, tending to their fishing nets.

"The people of Palestine, notwithstanding all its travails and misfortunes, still have undiminished faith in its future. And the people of Palestine know that the pathway to that future is the liberation of its homeland. . . . Only in the liberation of Palestine, spearheaded by Palestinians prepared to pay the price, can the supreme sacrifices of past generations of Palestinians be vindicated, and the visions and hopes of living Palestinians can be transformed into reality."

FAYEZ A. SAYEGH,
Palestinian refugee
spokesman, 1965

Palestinian leader Yasser Arafat

for taking a stand against what some perceived as the West's longstanding political influence in the Middle East. The Suez War planted a seed that would later bloom into further military action against Israel.

After 1956, Israelis enjoyed relative peace for the next 10 years, growing in many ways. Israel irrigated the dry Negev desert region, thereby increasing its agricultural production and income. More Jewish immigrants flooded the country, bringing new skills in such fields as engineering, medicine, and academics. Countries such as the U.S., eager to lend support to a fellow democratic nation, sent economic aid to Israel, while Arab countries such as Syria and Egypt received

an influx of military arms and supplies from America's superpower rival, the communist Soviet Union.

In the early 1960s, many pro-Palestinian organizations emerged, as the idea of Palestinian nationalism that had taken root prior to World War I swelled again. One group, the Palestinian Liberation Organization (PLO), was formed in 1964 with the stated goal of freeing the Palestinian homeland from the Israelis. Later, the group al-Fatah branched out from the PLO and called for a "movement for the liberation of Palestine." Yasser Arafat, a fiery young Palestinian studying in Cairo, emerged as al-Fatah's leader, and members of the group participated in

25

For almost 40 years, Yasser Arafat was a leading figure in Palestine, and even after his death in 2004, many Palestinians rallied around his image in support of al-Fatah.

raids into Israeli territory to disrupt industries and attack Israeli forces. For decades, up until his death in 2004, Arafat would be the leader of and spokesman for the Palestinian people.

Guerrilla attacks on Israeli territory increased by 1966, and in May 1967, Egyptian officials began a large build-up of troops, with Egypt, Jordan, and Syria positioning their forces to surround Israel. On June 5, 1967, war broke out as Israeli planes destroyed the jets of the Egyptian air force. Applying its strong air force and citizen army, Israel defeated Egypt and seized the Gaza Strip and the entire Sinai peninsula once again. On Israel's eastern border, Jordanians launched artillery attacks across the split city of Jerusalem into Israeli territory. In retaliation, Israel seized old Jerusalem and the West Bank. Israel also defeated Syria and acquired the territory known as the Golan Heights after fierce fighting. By June 10, the "Six-Day War" was over, and although Israel lost almost 800 soldiers (compared with about 4,000 Arab casualties), it had earned a resounding victory, expanding its size threefold. About 1.3 million Palestinians now lived under Israeli control.

Throughout the late 1960s and early '70s, the PLO and al-Fatah continued their armed struggle against Israel, and other violent pro-Palestinian groups also emerged. These groups began using tactics such as plane hijackings to publicize the Palestinian cause. At the 1972 Olympics in Munich,

After the Six-Day War in 1967, the UN passed Resolution 242, which called for Israel to return occupied territories to Palestinians and for the Palestinian refugee problem to be addressed. One of the resolution's main ideas was "land for peace." In exchange for the return of land, Israel would be assured peace. But the resolution went ignored. Later, the UN adopted Resolution 338, which reaffirmed the points made in Resolution 242. Resolutions 242 and 338 would emerge as common issues and sticking points in later peace talks between Israelis and Palestinians.

Despite the fact that the Golan Heights region was strongly fortified, Israel was able to conquer the area in only two days, leading Syrian troops to surrender to Israeli tanks.

The 1973 war between Israelis and Arabs occurred on days holy for both Jews and Muslims. The attack started on Yom Kippur, which many Jews consider their holiest day. On this day, a solemn occasion filled with prayer and fasting, also known as the Day of Atonement, Jews make amends for any wrongs or sins they've committed. During the war, Muslims were also in the midst of their holy month, Ramadan. Ramadan is a time for Muslims to reflect upon their religion and draw closer to God. During the month, people of the Islamic faith fast from dawn to sunset and seek to improve relationships with others.

Although Egypt and Syria surprised Israel with their Yom Kippur attack, they didn't take advantage of early victories, and Israel's military (above) soon overpowered them.

Germany, a group called Black September kidnapped and murdered 11 Israeli athletes. Only one year later, another war threatened to consume the volatile region. Still angered by their 1956 and 1967 defeats, Egyptians were hungry to regain power and compensate for their military humiliations. The new Egyptian president, Anwar al-Sadat, faced considerable unrest from the Egyptian public, which looked for its leader to do something about the Israeli situation.

A familiar story played out during the early 1970s as Israel and Egypt fortified their arsenals, with the world's competing superpowers providing missiles and guns to each: the Soviets supplying Egypt, and the Americans helping to arm Israel. In 1973, Egypt prepared to launch another attack against Israel with the help of Syria, which looked to regain the Golan Heights territory. On October 6, 1973, the two countries attacked Israel in what became known as the Yom Kippur War, named after the Jewish holiday on which it occurred. When a ceasefire was declared 18 days later, Israel emerged once again as the victor.

"After the 1967 war, . . . with the occupation of the West Bank and Gaza, it had hit home, literally. It was no longer my parents' legacy or an abstract historical or political concept. It became my burden, my responsibility. Overnight, I had become an 'exile,' and most of my family remained under occupation. The urge to go home became my overriding motivation. The era of resistance had taken on a new urgency and momentum. Thus began a momentous transition in my life in which activism was the key. I became involved in the growing Palestinian revolution."

HANAN ASHWARI, Palestinian politician, 1995

29

Many horrific and violent acts have occurred throughout the years at the hands of both Arabs and Jews. In one particularly dreadful episode, at the height of Israel's war with Lebanon in 1982, Israel allowed a group known as the Lebanese Christian Phalangist militia to enter the Palestinian refugee camps of Sabra and Shatila, near Beirut, in order to root out militants. Hundreds of refugees were murdered, including women and children. The Israeli defense minister at the time, Ariel Sharon, resigned amid the international fury. By the mid-1980s, the large number of Palestinian deaths in Lebanon had increased support and sympathy for the Palestinian cause worldwide.

Menachem Begin (left), Jimmy Carter (center), and Anwar al-Sadat won wide praise for the Camp David Accords; in 1978, Begin and al-Sadat received the Nobel Peace Prize.

After the Yom Kippur War, Israel and Egypt—wearied by war—finally sought a path to peace with the help of the U.S. On September 17, 1978, Egypt's al-Sadat and Israeli Prime Minister Menachem Begin signed a peace treaty known as the Camp David Accords (so named because talks were held at the U.S. presidential retreat of Camp David), with U.S. President Jimmy Carter looking on. The treaty laid out a plan to start peace talks and also provided the Palestinians some autonomy to rule on their own in areas occupied by Israelis. U.S. Secretary of State Henry Kissinger traveled to the Middle East several times to try to broker peace in the war-torn region.

Despite these efforts, violence continued to envelop Israel and Palestine. In the early 1980s, Israel waged war against its northern neighbor, Lebanon. Many Palestinians had moved to that country, and some launched attacks against Israel from Lebanese bases. In the late '80s, Palestinian youths, upset and frustrated after living their entire lives under Israeli control, started an intifada. They launched informal attacks against Israeli soldiers and citizens—some as mild as demonstrations and harassment, and others as deadly as riots, rock-throwing, and bombings using homemade explosives. But their weapons were no match for the tanks and automatic rifles possessed by Israel's well-trained military. Dozens of Israelis were killed by the attacks, while Israel's forceful retaliations resulted in the

الانتفاضة مستمرة
حتى القدس والاستقلال والعودة
الذكرى السنوية الأولى ٢٨ـ٩ـ٢٠٠١

INTIFADA

deaths of hundreds of Palestinians. The intifada spawned the formation of yet another militant Palestinian group called Hamas, which dedicated itself to the creation of an independent Palestine and the destruction of Israel.

The 1990s saw periods of both peace and fighting in the Middle East. In 1993, Arafat and Israeli Prime Minister Yitzhak Rabin signed an Israeli-PLO peace accord, which was promoted as a temporary first step toward Palestinian independence. Later that year, the same two leaders signed the Oslo Agreement, which provided for self-rule for Palestinians in Gaza and the West Bank. In 1994, words were put into action as Israelis started to withdraw from Gaza and the West Bank town of Jericho, ending 27 years of military occupation. And in 2000, Israel withdrew troops from Lebanon. The world wondered if peace might finally, actually, be at hand.

During the intifada—Arabic for "throwing off," as the Palestinians wanted to throw off Israeli rule—Palestinians met Israeli tanks with slingshots and other homemade weapons.

People on both sides of the Israeli-Palestinian conflict have resorted to acts of violence and murder to protest what they see as concessions to the other side, sometimes even perpetuating violence against their own people. The history of the conflict is peppered with assassinations of political leaders. President Anwar al-Sadat of Egypt was assassinated in 1981 by an Arab who was angered over Sadat's role in the 1978 Camp David Accords. And Israeli prime minister Yitzhak Rabin was killed in 1995, after attending a peace rally in Tel Aviv, by a fellow Jew who likewise opposed Rabin's efforts in the peace process.

A year after meeting with Yasser Arafat (left) in Gaza as another step toward Arab-Israeli peace, Yitzhak Rabin (right) became the only Israeli prime minister to be assassinated.

THE ISRAELI-PALESTINIAN CONFLICT

The potential peace deals—the Camp David Accords, the Israeli-PLO Peace Accord, and the Oslo Agreement—all fell by the wayside in September 2000, when a second intifada, the al-Aqsa intifada, began. Again, frustration among Palestinians exploded into a full-fledged uprising. It had been several years since Arafat and Rabin had signed the peace treaty, yet Palestinians saw little fulfillment in promises made. They still hadn't been granted any real authority, Jewish settlers still lived in predominantly Palestinian areas, and the prospect of peace faded.

Instead of throwing stones, as had been common in the 1980s intifada, Palestinians this time more frequently armed themselves with guns and homemade weapons, such as exploding bottles. As a group, Palestinians did not have a well-defined military; instead, attacks came in the form of individual assaults against Israeli targets. One of the most notorious tactics was the use of suicide bombers, in which men and women strapped explosives to their bodies under clothes, went to public places where Israeli civilians gathered, such as a market or bus, and blew themselves up. Israel often retaliated against such attacks with well-coordinated military assaults, hitting Palestinian militants with tanks and precise missile strikes. By 2006, an estimated 4,000 Palestinians had died in attacks since this renewal of fighting in 2000, and around 1,000 Israelis had been killed.

Ariel Sharon, an Israeli politician who for decades had advocated using military force against Israel's enemies, became the state's prime minister in

AN UNCERTAIN FUTURE

At the funeral of a Hamas leader, masked militants wore mock suicide bombs; suicide bombing is widely promoted in Palestine, including in music videos aimed at children.

Although the International Court of Justice called the West Bank border wall illegal, Israel went ahead with construction of the barrier, one-third of which was completed as of 2006.

2001 and vowed to crack down on the Palestinian insurgency. In 2002, Israeli tanks and troops poured into the West Bank and Palestinian settlements to subdue the uprising. Israel also began building a giant, 420-mile (670 km) wall along the West Bank border. The barrier was mostly a fence, but in some sections, a concrete wall stood tall and strong. Israelis hoped the wall would reduce attacks, but the barricade angered many Palestinians, as it restricted their access to work, schools, hospitals, and farmland, and Israel came under international criticism for the barrier. Israel also pounded Arafat's compound in Ramallah with gunfire and tank shells for five solid weeks in 2002 in hopes of compelling him to rein in Palestinian militants. Although Arafat was the leader of the Palestinian people and the 1994 winner of the Nobel Peace Prize, many critics throughout the world contended he didn't do enough to stop the suicide bombings and other Palestinian attacks.

Further ideas for peace emerged during this tumultuous time. In 2003, the U.S., now led by President George W. Bush, issued a plan called a "road map" for peace, which included a timetable for reducing Palestinian violence and limiting Israeli military excursions and settlement activity in Palestinian areas. Following the road map plan, in 2004, Israel announced a plan for the withdrawal of a few small settlements in Gaza and the West Bank, along with the Israeli troops who protected them. Just as the Palestinians didn't want to leave their homes decades before, Israeli settlers didn't want to abandon their homes, either. In 2005, Israeli troops had to forcibly remove 8,000 settlers from their homes in scenes that were often emotional.

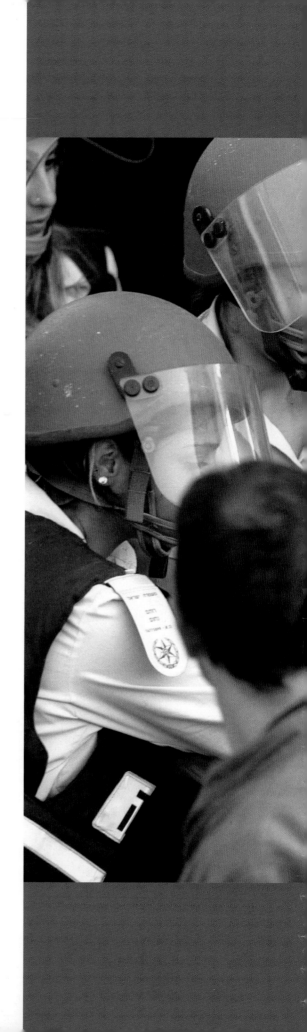

Israeli police evicted dozens of Israeli settlers living illegally in a West Bank Palestinian home in 2006, but not before some settlers had thrown explosives at the officers.

In November 2004, Arafat died in a Paris hospital, leaving a void in Palestinian leadership. Then, in early 2006, in the Palestinian national elections, the militant group Hamas swept to power in a surprising political victory. Israel and the worldwide community watched nervously as Hamas—an avowed enemy of Israel—took unprecedented power. The Israelis, too, had new leadership, as Sharon was incapacitated by a massive stroke in 2006. While the new Israeli government, led by Prime Minister Ehud Olmert, vowed to continue withdrawing settlers, it refused to work with Hamas, which it—along with the U.S. and much of the West—considered a terrorist organization. The ultimate ramifications of Hamas's empowerment might not be known for years.

What is known, however, is that this conflict continues to affect the daily lives of Palestinians and Israelis alike, hanging over them like a black cloud. Palestinians still live without a formal state. The founding of Israel in 1948, referred to as *al-Nakba*, or "the catastrophe," by Palestinians, haunts them to this day; many feel displaced and resent the fact that their ancestral homes were destroyed. Palestinians find it hard to move from

"For nearly four decades, he expressed and symbolized in his person the national aspirations of the Palestinian people. Now that he is gone, both Israelis and Palestinians, and the friends of both peoples throughout the world, must make even greater efforts to bring about the peaceful realization of the Palestinian right of self-determination."

UN SECRETARY-GENERAL KOFI ANNAN, after the death of Palestinian leader Yasser Arafat, November 2004

41

one place to another, especially if they have to cross the border from Palestinian territory into Israel for work or school. Until recently, even in traditional Palestinian territories such as Gaza, they have had to live side-by-side with Israelis.

Israelis, meanwhile, constantly worry about their security. They are Jews living in the middle of a vast expanse of Arab territories, many hostile, on all sides. While in public—shopping for clothes, riding a bus, or going to a movie—they can never be certain of their safety. They fear that either more Palestinians will join current anti-Israel organizations or that new and more violent ones will form. Israel's economy benefits from throngs of tourists, especially religious pilgrims visiting this holy land, but the new wave of intifada in 2000 triggered a decline in tourism.

The world worries, too, that this regional conflict may feed into more widespread violence across the globe. In a way, the world's security is linked to security for Israelis and Palestinians. Political alliances are often seen in general terms. Like schoolchildren choosing sides on a playground, countries around the world are widely perceived to be on one side or another. Many Arabs view the U.S., Britain, and other Western nations as Israeli allies, which sparks anti-Western sentiment among some Middle Eastern nations. Even the feelings of hatred behind the September 11, 2001, terrorist attacks upon the U.S. could be linked, at least in part, to the perception that the U.S. is pro-Israeli, and therefore anti-Arab. In turn, some Westerners have a hard time separating most Arabs from the few fanatics who perpetuate violence against the West in the name of Allah (God

In addition to militant groups, there are about 30,000 official security forces within Palestine, among them border police, military police, and a presidential security unit.

"We are sacrificing our lives here. I saw one woman . . . she lost her son. She said she would sacrifice all her sons for our statehood. People are saying they want their statehood, they say they will do it by peace, but if peace doesn't work, they will sacrifice their lives."

ASHRAF ABU-SHABAN, Palestinian shopkeeper, 2000

of the Muslim faith). The images of Palestinians dancing in the streets after September 11 created ill feelings among some in the West.

The Israeli-Palestinian conflict today remains complex and highly controversial, as it has for decades. In this often-bloody face-off, both sides claim a historic right to the land. Both sides maintain they are justified in their actions, and both claim the role of victim. Jews point to the Holocaust and centuries of persecution as reason enough to have their own state as told in the Bible. Palestinians speak of decades of oppression that have occurred since Israel was created and want their land and homes returned. When two sides are so passionately at odds, there will always be two versions to the story. Arguments persist in who was the aggressor in any given conflict and who was the victim, and what the reasons were for war or deadly attacks. Body counts already in the thousands on each side continue to rise with each new wave of violence.

"I will speak to you about the reasons behind these [September 11] incidents. I will honestly tell you about the minutes in which the decision was made so that you will consider. I say to you that God knows that the idea of striking the towers never occurred to us. But, after things had gone too far and we saw the injustice of the U.S.-Israeli alliance against our people in Palestine and Lebanon, I started thinking of that. The events that influenced me directly trace back to 1982 and subsequent events when the United States gave permission to the Israelis to invade Lebanon. . . ."

OSAMA BIN LADEN, Al Qaeda terrorist leader, October 2004

Despite the seemingly endless strife, Israelis and Palestinians today go about their everyday lives, doing

44

People around the world have taken sides in the Israeli-Palestinian conflict; in 2005, Pakistani children stood on Israeli and U.S. flags in protest of the two countries.

Throughout the Israeli-Palestinian conflict, people on both sides have witnessed countless funerals, and many wonder how many more lives will be lost before the violence ends.

what people all over the world do—going to work, dining with loved ones, strolling in the cool of the evening. It's just that they do so with a heightened state of alertness, with the knowledge that an attack can happen at any moment. They wonder if they—or their children or grandchildren—will ever see peace. While many long to leave the past behind and work toward a brighter future, others find previous transgressions hard to forget. And so Palestinians continue their struggle to recoup their ancestral homelands, while Israelis fight for the right to live unmolested in The Promised Land. Two peoples, two different goals, one land.

47

BIBLIOGRAPHY

Bickerton, Ian J., and Carla L. Klausner. *A Concise History of the Arab-Israeli Conflict.*
Englewood Cliffs, N.J.: Prentice Hall, 1995.

Gelvin, James L. *The Israel-Palestine Conflict: One Hundred Years of War.*
New York: Cambridge University Press, 2005.

Harms, Gregory, and Todd Ferry. *The Palestine-Israel Conflict: A Basic Introduction.*
London: Pluto Press, 2005.

The Israeli-Palestinian Conflict: Crisis in the Middle East.
New York: Reuters, 2002.

Laqueur, Walter, and Barry Rubin, eds. *The Israel-Arab Reader.*
New York: Penguin Books, 1995.

Senker, Cath. *The Arab-Israeli Conflict.*
North Mankato, Minn.: Smart Apple Media, 2004.

INDEX